My Soul
SHOUTS!

My Soul SHOUTS!

the spiritual wisdom of
BISHOP ANDERSON

To Ava Mintz — May you always know the love of Christ. God keep you always & for ever.

6/6/03

VINTON RANDOLPH ANDERSON
with selections from vivienne l. anderson

JUDSON PRESS

valley forge

My Soul Shouts! The Spiritual Wisdom of Bishop Anderson
© 2002 by Judson Press, Valley Forge, PA 19482-0851
All rights reserved.

Bible quotations in this volume are from the New Revised Standard
Version of the Bible, copyright © 1989 by the Division of Christian
Education of the National Council of the Churches of Christ in the
United States of America. Used by permission. All rights reserved.

Library of Congress Cataloging-in-Publication data
available upon request. 800-222-3872, ext. 2128

Printed in Canada

08 07 06 05 04 03

10 9 8 7 6 5 4 3 2

contents

Part I: Of the Nature of God

Part IV: Of the Human Condition and Destiny

Part V: Of Prayer and Contemplation

Part VI: Of Salvation and Human Sin

Part VII: Of Social Justice and Outreach

foreword

hroughout the past thirty years of my own
service in the ordained ministry, I have
nurtured a special interest in the history and
leadership of the African Methodist Episcopal
Church, even though most of my service has been as
a United Methodist. It is well known that the A.M.E.
Church has provided seminal prophetic leadership in
insisting upon the uplift of African Americans and
persons of African descent. Accordingly, I quickly
became an admiring "cousin" of many of the men
and women—from Richard Allen and Jarena Lee to
Henry McNeal Turner and my former student Vashti
McKenzie—who have distinguished themselves in
the A.M.E. Church from its inception to the present
day. More than two decades ago, I took notice of one
A.M.E. leader who seemed to be emerging as a great
apostle of ecumenism on the world scene. The name
of that person is Vinton Anderson.

Over the years, I continued to keep abreast of his vision for ministry, his concern for quality African American theological education, and his passion for justice that seemed to parallel the great tradition established by a number of his A.M.E. forebears. When many of us within the boundaries of the A.M.E. Second Episcopal District (which includes Washington, D.C.) learned six years ago that Vinton Anderson was to be the new bishop for this area, no one was more publicly delighted than I. Somehow, I knew that finally I would get an opportunity to work with him as a partner in theological education. I also hoped that I would benefit from wise counsel. Little did I know that he would take me under his wing, welcoming critical dialogue and affording experiences that would bring me closer than ever to the forward thrust of the church's witness in the nation's capital.

Early in the new millennium, Bishop Anderson began to share some of his writings with me and asked me for comments. Beginning with segments of his master's thesis on Reinhold Niebuhr years ago, these writings extended to speeches and denominational booklets, and then moved to articles and short reflections and meditations. It did not take long for me to note the special quality of his mind and the genuineness of his gift and concern that, while well grounded in the black religious experience, extended a considerable distance beyond to include the whole sweep of the human experience. The writings displayed a time-honored respect for the learned ministry, without the loftiness and detachment that often accompanies such values. In Vinton Anderson, I have found the vocational commitment of a church leader who has truly shown himself to be "a man for all seasons"!

Of all the writings and musings that Bishop Anderson shared with me, I found myself returning again and again to his short reflective meditations, drawn from his personal journal. These seem to capture the diverse and captivating moments in which one becomes inspired to pause in our "God talk" and invite a new kind of conversation with God. Bishop Anderson's meditations seemed to invite me into that conversation about the human condition, its odd challenges, and the splendid ways that God through Jesus Christ seeks to mediate all the while, if allowed. It became clear that these short meditations had to be published. This is the genesis of *My Soul Shouts!*

The thought-provoking vignettes within this book are nicely arranged in themes that help one to appreciate the theological contours of Bishop Anderson's faith journey. Yet he has not been on this journey alone! As indicated by the occasional poetic commentaries by Vivienne, his wife of fifty years, the bishop has truly been blessed not just by a "help mate" but by a remarkable *soul mate* as well. Vivienne Anderson's brief commentaries are strategically dispersed through the book and appear as periodic companion pieces to the topics on which Bishop

Anderson's attention has been riveted. In this way, the book indicates the way in which Anderson's career has truly vertical and horizontal coordinates of support, yielding a leadership style dedicated to God—through Jesus Christ, the church, and the global community, as well as through Bishop Anderson's race, his nation, and his family.

Readers of this book are in for a treat as they, too, are invited to join the conversation with God clearly taking place within these pages. I count it all joy to have had a confirming "second opinion" role in moving the early drafts of this anthology along the pathway to the production of this book. (Indeed, I am grateful for the nudges—at times not so gentle—by Mrs. Jackie Dupont-Walker, the bishop's devoted executive aide, who would not hesitate to call me at odd hours to remind me of deadlines and the need to value the bishop's time! Anyone who has worked on a book knows that such focused reminders are necessary if the project is ever to see the light of day as a finished work.) I am delighted to recommend this book, which has inspired my soul to shout as well.

CAIN HOPE FELDER, PH.D.
Professor of New Testament Language and Literature
Howard University, School of Divinity
Washington, D.C.

*M*y *Soul Shouts!* is a collection of vignettes from my journal (which covers several years) and includes eight original poems by my earthly soul mate, Vivienne, who has shared my experiences for above a half-century. We have each known joy and pain in every segment of life, but we have been sustained by our unrelenting devotion to the work of Christ and by our love for each other.

In our partnership we have never insinuated ourselves into the lives of others, but we have also carefully avoided the tendency to look through them. We have striven to engage in meaningful relationships consisting of more than surface encounters, and the result has been genuine friendships.

Moving beyond the trivial and the casual to the challenging demands of reflective observation causes one to live in the shoes of another, and more so, interlocks experiences at the deepest level. Hopefully, these meanderings will stimulate a curiosity to look beyond what appears to be in the world around, while attempting to measure in some form the ethos and pathos that could motivate another's life.

On our golden wedding anniversary, Vivienne and I dedicate these pages to those we hold in unyielding affection and to others unknown to us in search of soul kinship, whose affection would have enriched our lives. Our souls shout in a harmony of thanksgiving and celebration, while we rejoice that we hold this milestone in common with some and as a sign of hope for others. Perhaps those who reflect with us in these pages will be reminded of moments in their own lives that evoke shouts from the soul.

—VRA

acknowledgments

This book represents years of reflection and notations gathered from my personal journals and occasional papers. First, let me express my deep appreciation to my dear help meet, Vivienne, who has contributed immeasurably to this publication by adding a handful of her poetic selections. Even more, she is inextricably connected to every thought I have composed. My habit of journaling had its genesis in her encouragement, and the rest can be read in and between the lines.

A special word of thanks to my friend, Cain Hope Felder, is in order. From his first glance at my notes, he showed genuine excitement. I was particularly pleased when he agreed to serve as the principle critic in my development of this manuscript.

My executive aide, Jacquelyn Dupont-Walker, deserves abundant kudos for her extraordinary devotion and initiative in assuring that the work, down to the smallest detail, was done in an efficient and timely manner.

Of course, I am grateful to those at Judson Press for their kind and thorough handling of this project.

Last, thanks to all of the people who contributed to this work by permitting me to be in their situations. They opened avenues for me to think about thinking.

—VRA

M y soul shouts and only senses the motion of other souls as it relates to God. I have long felt that humankind is quadripartite—that is we are body, mind, heart, and soul: four levels of existence. Aside from my own experiences, which seem to validate that these four levels of existence are reality, I have taken refuge in Jesus' words in Mark 12:30: "You shall love the Lord your God with all your heart, and with all your soul, and with all your mind, and with all your strength."

The *body*, that physical and primordial existence which can be tortured and mutilated by ourselves and other humans, performs the physical and sensual acts and therefore knows both pleasure and pain. The *mind*, the psyche where the intellect has its seat and which is capable of genius, carries out the rational aspects of our being. However, it is also subject to manipulation and to imperfect thoughts. The *heart* is that feeling self where emotions are harbored. It is that super sense, the emotional conduit that links us with other humans and assures us there is a person, a presence beyond us. But the heart, too, is often tantalized and subject to temptations. The *soul*, which is that indestructible essence, is in deep isolation from other persons and from their ability to communicate with it.

Only God can communicate with the soul; no human can reach this deepest level of being. No harm can befall the soul, because it is the seat of our immortality. It is the soul that finds its escape from all that's mortal, but can never find release from its Maker. The soul is that indescribable reliability that bears the image of the eternal and that has its being in its attachment to the immutable sovereignty which has created it. It has the capacity to wait, to generate dynamic and holy quietness, because it has all eternity to be in sync with its creator.

The soul has no power to act but is the receiving entity of the person who waits in meditation on its God. The soul is that part of me which cannot be buffeted by the external viciousness of an ambitious world or by a restless and anxious self. Only God can touch the soul! God alone can find it and feed it.

We are all living souls, and in that reality alone we are indestructible. The body may collapse, the mind may deteriorate, the heart may be frustrated, but the soul remains serene—waiting, needing us to be quiet, so there is an awakened consciousness that God is present and speaking and possessing.

At our demise, the returning of our ashes to the ground, it is the soul which continues in existence beyond this place of uncertainty, corruption, and brokenness. The soul is not limited to occasions, time, and space. It is the wings of our existence. *My Soul Shouts!* is about the self whose soul is in search of the righteous ground of a loving God and who knows its place in heavenly company.

The soul is, as my ancestors have testified in the face of turbulent testing, "anchored in the Lord." So my soul shouts in a language other humans cannot interpret, but it is a sound that echoes the melody of the eternal and that creates a harmony which connects me to other souls.

In the black experience and in many other religious contexts, the *shout* is not a detached phenomenon; it is an emotional response growing out of frustration and tribulation and sometimes joy, but ultimately it is an outward sign of an inward hope. I am convinced that the shout resonates far deeper than the echo heard and that it can be an authentic outer expression of inner yearnings.

If an individual is genuinely spontaneous in responding to the vibrations of the soul, that person cannot resist an outward pouring of the sensation she or he is experiencing. It must also be acknowledged that shouting from that level of being needs no manipulation of outward circumstances, because its source is internal and eternal. "When the spirit hits you, shout hallelujah!"—or be still and know that God is God.

The nature of my musings in this compendium will indicate that the shouts of my soul have come mainly in my moments of private reflection, not in my frequent participation in public worship. There have been many times when I have experienced outward bursts of joy, but I am never so fulfilled as when I have felt the purging, wrenching of the soul in the silence of deep reflection. My soul was shouting!

It's all right to shout—but much more so when the shout is hooked to the real thing. When we contemplate how God has acted in our lives to deliver us from our human no-win situations, we can do no other than to give God praise.

How and where and when this explosion of the spirit takes place and by what manner it is made manifest, we must always wish for a validation of that event through an inward quest of the soul. The journey inward is the only protection from the bias of outward opinion, for only the self knows whether the shout is a tear or a smile.

I publish these vignettes from my personal journal to share those times when my soul was shouting, "Be still, and know that I am God" (Psalm 46:10).

PROLOGUE

from divinity to devotion

In him we live and move and have our being
(Acts 17:28).

In this generation, as we gather as a community of
faith, we are fully aware of the ominous forebodings
that push our world closer to the edge of annihila-
tion, a condition of both international and domestic
consequence. Amid this predicament, the real problem for the church is not whether our faith is sufficient, but how it can be more relevant to contemporary life and its urgent needs. Progress can happen
only if we are fully conscious of our God-like estate
and if we are willing to test the available unexploited
resources in the face of strong adversaries. Our
marching orders must be centered around an affirmation of God's sovereignty in this world.

Acts 17:28 is the Pauline response to the pagan
religions and godless philosophies so prevalent in his

day. Paul, uninhibited by the accusation that he was an intellectual scavenger, proclaims that God is the very source of our existence—that the principles of life and motion come from God. The text postulates at least two crucial issues pertinent to our thinking: (1) a reaffirmation of divine presence in the human equation, and (2) the response which divinity generates in the human spirit.

Now I have no intention of making an argument for the existence of God in this volume, nor do I believe it necessary to delineate the divine attributes. I am reasonably certain that we can ignore the atheists of the last century who dissected human bodies and demanded "show me the soul." We are surely not shaken by the Russian cosmonaut who, while spinning dizzily around the earth, bragged, "I don't see God anywhere up here." Although we may discover that God is not the Being we once thought God to be, that discovery does not mean that God does not exist. The God I came to know in Sunday school fifty-five years ago is not the same God under whose dominion my life is now controlled. However, my fundamental understanding of God has not altered from then till now.

What does disturb me greatly is the overwhelming confusion which persists about God, and the relationship of humankind to God's purposes. What of the divine presence in the human equation? To me it follows as night the day: If God is divine, and he is, then we who are made in God's image have in us the pattern of divinity—the quality of being "a little lower than God" (Psalm 8:5, NRSV). Divinity in this sense is not a title of preeminence for humankind; it is a sign of mutuality and respect and responsibility. Something is asked of us as human beings that is not expected of other creatures: "You have given them dominion over the works of your hands; you have put all things under their feet" (Psalm 8:6). What, then, is implied in personhood?

Three other questions flow from this inquiry for the amplification of our pursuit: (1) What does it mean to be human in our interior makeup? (2) What is the person in relationship to God? (3) What is the person in relationship to the world God has created?

In answer to the first question, the Hebrews understood a person to be a unity of matter and spirit, and the combination of the two makes a soul, or a living being (Genesis 2:7). Hebrew thought admitted that body or flesh is subject to corruption and fallibility, but that it is not in itself evil or corrupt—not naturally evil. Thus, when I am in full communion with the Almighty, I feel good even in my natural body; it gets all over—I feel good, good, good! The New Testament summarizes it for us: that the whole of a human being is God's creation; our body is a temple.

Questions two and three—What is our relationship to God? and What is our relationship to God's creation?—are answered in Genesis 1:27. The person is represented as the crown and climax of God's activity, "made in the image of God." We understand this to mean that humankind was intended to have dominion over the other living creatures on earth just as God exercises rule over our humanity. Consequently, we are not to sink to the level of beasts, functioning as predators or parasites, consuming and destroying one another other. We are children of the Most High and must bear the image of the heavenly Father. And if there is a problem discerning the shape of that image, "look to Jesus now and live!" And as God's creatures, we are expected to give God dominion over our lives—or putting it another way, to give our lives to God. That's devotion! We are inherently divine; we are potentially devout. The eternal mandate to the human spirit is to actualize our potential—to go from divinity to devotion.

Let us now engage the other main issue: the response which God generates in the human spirit. This response is about visualizing what God intended for us from creation. And how does the vision come? I suggest three ways. First, by living creatively in God's world—open to truth, receptive to revelation, and believing in the divine potential for our lives. We will not get the vision if we are confined to our own little worlds—of business and politics, of family and recreation—the little worlds in which we live and move, and are ultimately powerless.

Cosmic security is achieved when our egos are submerged and our adulation is raised.

Second, our understanding of God's vision for us grows deeper by living under God's grace. It is under grace that we learn the secret of being God's child. Under grace we come to know companionship unlike any other, walking with Jesus through the changing scenes of an unpredictable sojourn, knowing full well that the one who dwells in the secret place of the Most High will abide under the shadow of the Almighty. Paul lays claim to that grace. While a casualty of human tragedy he survives with dignity and hears heaven announce, "My grace is sufficient."

Finally, we understand God's vision when we begin to manifest it by engaging in Christ's service. Our shouts and our hallelujahs and our amens won't do it alone: "Not everyone who says to me 'Lord, Lord' will enter the kingdom of heaven, but only the one who does the will of my Father" (Matthew 7:21). And again, "What does the Lord require of you, but to do justice, and to love kindness, and to walk humbly with your God?" (Micah 6:8). We are to respond to the crying needs of an oppressed, afflicted, and dying people—to be at the cutting edge of contemporary struggles as advocates and mediators for human rights! "Make a joyful noise," but also "serve the Lord with gladness."

We may not know the wide scope of God's purposes nor be able to define God's ways, but we will

know when our works and witness are related to God. We will know when we've done right despite our humanness, because in us is that divine spark of transcendence and the capacity to move from divinity to devotion. "Beloved, we are God's children now; what we will be has not yet been revealed. What we do know is this: when he is revealed, we will be like him" (1 John 3:2). To know who we are, whose we are, and whom we serve is to move from divinity to devotion.

PART I

of the nature of GOD

A HEALING

Today I had a prodigious walk on the treadmill. I had never walked as far or as long. I experienced this great acceleration of energy, and I felt I could go as long as I desired. I kept trudging when all of a sudden something happened! It was not a physical thing nor a mundane intrusion. It was far more profound.

It was an engagement at the soul level. There was the inner voice, speaking clear and precise: "You are not omnipotent. This sensation you are feeling is about your healing and not about titillating your ego. You know the race is not given to the swift; your moment of exhilaration is the result of an enduring obedience to live a different lifestyle, which is more attuned to God's prescription for your healing."

And I felt this shout in my soul. God had healed my body of cardiac disease, and it was time for me to do a new thing. I sensed that God now wanted me to participate in a more pervasive healing ministry. It all has to do with the ways I have had to readjust my life, my thinking and acting, and my attitude. All of these have been tempered through soul encounters.

Since the early 1980s this new revelation has moved me beyond what God had done in my life to what God *is* doing and *will* do. So as my soul looks back, I no longer wonder how I got over. My soul has been shouting, "It is a work of God!"

A SHOUT FOR MOM

I returned home to Bermuda in 1972 following my election as bishop in the African Methodist Episcopal Church, and I could hardly wait to announce that Ruth Anderson's son was now a bishop.

It was important for me to say it that way because my mother had been unwed when I was born some forty-four years earlier. Mom herself had not lived to celebrate with me the great distance God had brought us.

I was standing in the pulpit at Allen Temple A.M.E. Church in Somerset, the church where I had first answered the call to preach, in the community where my mother had enjoyed few pleasures and much pain. I just wanted to shout my achievement for her sake—and to her memory.

Something good had come out of my "untimely birth" (see 1 Corinthians 15:8), and that which had come to me belonged also to her.

AROUND AND AROUND

At the amusement park with family members, I watched the little ones who were thoroughly thrilled, enjoying their ride on the merry-go-round.

That particular day it struck me that the merry-go-round has been turning for generations. It may have different shapes and varying symbols and motifs in different places, but one thing is consistent: it keeps going around and around. While it will express a variety of forms of aesthetic beauty, its going-aroundness continues to amuse and delight countless numbers who ride on it throughout the world.

It is this consistency, this essence of unity, and this never-changing sameness which draws people to its movement that fascinate me. The merry-go-round's continuity of endless aroundness reminds me of that enduring dependability of the "first cause" —God who compels all into eternal movement with purpose and pleasure of the soul.

So it is for all who continue the quest for true movement and who never cease to search for this consistency. They will discover that the "immovable mover" never moves but is forever the same.

The author of the Epistle to the Hebrews reminds us, Jesus Christ never changes; he is the same yesterday, today, and forever (Hebrews 13:8). And the psalmist said, Trust God at all times, for God is our refuge (Psalm 62:8).

FORTUNATE INDEED

Today I had a flashback to a Saturday afternoon in March on the Eastern Airline shuttle from New York to Washington, D.C. The flashback was the memory of the great silence and the deep consternation reflected on the faces of fellow passengers following a loud explosion while we were in flight.

What had happened? All I knew was that the sound was unlike anything I had ever heard on the many flights I had taken in my lifetime. So, for a brief period I gathered my wits and my courage and began to pray, believing the inevitable was upon us. Shortly afterward an explanation came from the pilot: "Lightning hit the plane. We have checked the instruments and find everything normal. Fortunately our electrical system was not damaged." The pilot then added a postscript, I suppose for our comfort: "These planes are built to withstand such a shock."

I thought to myself, "That pilot was right the first time. We were fortunate, not because the plane was built well but because the lightning did not devastate the system." For, even after the pilot's words, we remained prayerful until the touch down. We knew who the real Pilot was, and so we said "Thank God!" as we applauded the landing.

GOD RISES EARLY

We were on a vacation cruise with friends along the West Coast from San Francisco via Canada to Alaska. One morning on awakening, I perceived the beauty about us was so clearly a sign of God's presence that I commented at breakfast, "God gets up awfully early!"

God must, of necessity, rise early in order to monitor human ambition and counter human schemes. It takes a God fully awake to oversee a creation so enormous and complex and with creatures so varied, especially those who are human.

God is so fully God, that God has numbered every hair on every head. Nothing escapes God's attention. God hardly sleeps, and yet God rises early!

IMMORTALITY

"Titus and Jackie had another girl!" my wife, Vivienne, announced when she opened the mail the other day. Her words seemed strange because Titus had been killed in a car accident months earlier. Jackie had been seven months pregnant when Titus "put on" immortality. In the wake of the tragedy, it became clear that some part of the divine intention was for Titus' immortality to precede his departure from mortality. The new baby, Tia, is as much a part of Titus in his death as she was in his life, which reveals powerfully that in life or death, our children are an inseparable part of us because we and they are forever one with the Eternal.

IN SOLITUDE

When I am in solitude with nature, with sky, mountain, river, sea, and tree, all merge into one.

And when there are no houses or tall buildings, no paved roads or mechanical instruments or vehicles visible to the naked eye, but only animals, birds, fish, and lofty thoughts, my soul merges with nature in harmony with God and eternity.

"And God said, let the water teem with living creatures, and let the birds fly above the earth across the expanse of the sky" (Genesis 1:20, NIV).

AUTUMN

What beauty bursts upon our sight
What glorious hues of mixed delight
Blaze forth in glory from the leaves
That autumn paints and deftly weaves
In brilliant golds and browns and reds!

What skill is this with gentle brush
Adorns the fall in shameless blush?
What mind, what spirit can devise
Such splendor for our earthly eyes
And cause our souls to soar on high?

It is the Master's touch that blends
All things that he in mercy sends,
To show his love in special ways
To lengthen and complete our days,
That we in glory, too, may shine.

—VIVIENNE L. ANDERSON

LIVING FOREVER

We often wish we could explain reality through the scientific method and discover eternity within human achievement, because the spiritual ground of existence is far more complex than the most extravagant scientific theory can postulate. After all, "Has not God made foolish the wisdom of the world?" (1 Corinthians 1:20).

In the end, it is not what is believable that matters, but what is believed. Our eternality is in our complete surrender to an infinite God who has promised everlasting life in response to our faith, which Jesus has said could be the size of a mustard seed (Matthew 17:20).

MAMA SAW A RAINBOW

Mama is one of the exceptional people in God's world, and she is now in her eighties. One Christmas, this alert lady shared with us about her trip by train from St. Louis to Portland last summer. Her face lit up as she said, "One evening I saw a rainbow. The colors were so vivid, and it followed our trail for a great distance." It seemed that for Mama that rainbow was a sign of God's enduring presence, and its beauty evidence of God's creative wonder. She carries that memory of that magnificent symbol, and it fortifies her conviction that God guides those who journey by faith. At Christmastime, that rainbow was Mama's testimony of God's surrounding presence in the coming of Jesus to bring salvation.

NO BETTER THAN OTHERS

God does not favor me, but God does allow me to be a part of that stream which is of eternal value. God leads me in the flow of goodness only because I choose to enter the waters of God's righteousness, and risk a safe passage predicted by God's laws for the universe. So, even when the quiet stream turns to rapids and I am dashed about, even if I am broken up, that which remains is me—the me in God's likeness. I know that to be the way, because Jesus on the cross, broken and bleeding, thirsting and praying to the Father, never ceased to be the God image. We overcome not because we are better than others but because the rivers of our trouble finally flow into an eternal sea.

ON KNOWING GOD

The key to my hotel room is some kind of magnetic disc, and it has no visible number identifying the room. However, in the coffee shop there is an ultraviolet lamp that reveals the otherwise hidden number. The hostess let me see my room number on my disc. It was an interesting revelation, but I was surprised at how the number was inscribed—in an unsophisticated scribble. What I gathered from that demonstration was a new sense of the presence of that number. By looking hard and carefully I could now see it even with the naked eye.

I realized, "Now I see it because I am conscious of its presence, and I can also discern the form of its existence." Similarly, when I am conscious of God's presence, I know that God exists. Yet, greater than this is when I feel God on the inside. Inside this earthly vessel, my soul shouts!

PREOCCUPIED

It was precisely 8:30 A.M. when I arrived at the gate and sat next to my friend who was making a trip to Los Angeles with me. He was so preoccupied with his reading that he did not see me, and for a while I felt invisible. When he finished underlining certain portions of his book, he glanced around—and even at me—but still was unaware of my presence. Perhaps by then his own mental defense would not allow him to believe that such a thing could happen—that I could have been sitting at his side all along. He then got up and walked away, again looking anxiously around, apparently with some consternation about my whereabouts. By then, I would not have dared to insinuate myself by attracting his attention. So near and yet so far!

At 8:55 my friend finally spotted me. He must have been at peace with the world and assured of God's protecting presence, to have had another person so close by and not to have been cautious enough to take note of who I was or what threat I might have posed.

The little drama made me wonder how often we are looking for God when God is present already.

THE FIRE CAME

When the fire came I am not sure I handled it well. It happened at the building where I had an office in St. Louis, and I was out of town at the time. Upon my return and discovery of the destruction, I really did not want to deal with the agony of loss. After all, no one had been hurt. But many of my possessions had gone up in smoke. Historical documents, plaques and citations, and memorabilia were destroyed in the fire, and I did not want to count the loss. I did not even want to revisit the location, and it was months before I could bring myself to do so.

I needed to start over again, and that for me was a profound understatement. Friends helped me to locate and move into another facility, and I settled in again. However, pondering the treasures consumed in the fire left a gnawing sensation of disappointment. For a long time, I remained aloof from that personal tragedy.

Years have gone by now, and I know that much of what was taken in the fire has been given back to me in so many ways. Providence has its own way of repositioning our vantage point. At that tick of the watch, the fire that came might well have been in the providence of God.

THE DOVE AND THE BEAR

Recently I heard a moving testimony by an eloquent lady called Dovey. She has served the church capably and faithfully through the years. Her craft and gifts have been cherished, but her testimony that day was humble and assuring. She confided in us that she was losing her sight, but it was evident she was not in despair. Coming to retirement she was prepared to see through the darkness.

Following Dovey's witness I heard the news of "Bear" Bryant's demise. He had only recently announced his retirement as football coach for the University of Alabama, and in that arena his name was, and is, legend. How ironic that at the culmination of a glowing career, death's darkness ushered him into eternal light.

The contrast between these lives struck me powerfully. A "Dove," standing before a few church leaders saying, "The time for my replacement is at hand," and the "Bear," his retirement announcement a national media event anticipating a bright future. One was preparing for blindness; the other at last could see. How strange are the turns along the way of life, but how reassuring to know in the end, darkness and light are the same to God.

WISHFUL THINKING

Is wishful thinking the progenitor of hope? Hope does often become reality, I observed.

This notion came as a result of my seven-year-old grandchild, Natina, inquiring about her ancestry—particularly about my mother. "Who was she? How old is she? Where is she?" came the rapid barrage of questions.

Well, my mother had been deceased for forty-eight years. So my methodology for answering was meticulous for this inquisitive mind.

"My mother was Ruth Anderson. If she were alive she would be 94. Great-grand Webster (my mother-in-law, whom Natina knows) is 92."

"Wow," Natina said. "She'd almost be a hundred." And then she began the count, "Ninety-four, ninety-five, ninety-six, ninety-seven, ninety-eight, ninety-nine, one hundred."

Then she stopped to look at me and ask, "How old are you, Paw Paw?"

I said, "Seventy-three."

Natina might have retorted, "Wow, you're old too!" Instead, she said, "You've got a long way to go before you reach ninety-nine."

This was a moment of soul encounter for me, and I wondered, had God's providence set her thoughts to hope or was this wishful thinking on her part?

PART II

of the person and
work of JESUS CHRIST

A NEW BODY

My young friend, in his mid-thirties, had experienced the sudden death of his wife. I could tell he was agonizing about her untimely departure. He was seeking answers to quiet his soul. At one point, he asked me about what body we have in a new world.

No doubt there are those who believe our new bodies will be an extension of the present, but in answering my young friend, I rebutted that belief. I am convinced it would be an injustice for God to lift me up in the new life with the old body. Having had so much pain and discomfort in this frame, my hope is to be free from the limitations of this ruptured tent. Christ returned with wounds for Thomas to see and touch (John 20:26-27), but they were not the bleeding wounds of the crucifixion. They were made on the cross but healed in the resurrection.

Hallelujah! A new body for a new world.

ADMIT IT

The night I saw *Superman II*, I concluded that in all things religion is affirmed.

In distress and devoid of power, the ordinary person admits failure and petitions a greater power for renewal and regeneration. A caring and benevolent being recognized by humanity as sovereign always responds. In the movie *Superman*, the light received from Kryptonite transformed the ordinary Clark Kent into a superhero with previously unimagined powers. Then, being fully under supernatural influence, this inherently ordinary person discovered his enemy to be manageable.

So is the "ordinary" Christian capable of overcoming. Our light is the Christ, and the darkness cannot put it out.

"The light shines in the darkness, and the darkness did not overcome it" (John 1:5).

HUMAN AND DIVINE

As human beings, we were created and called to become our best selves—but not by succumbing to the false pride of humanism. Humanism asserts that we are capable of maximizing our human potential in and of ourselves; humanism negates the need for and existence of God—in effect by claiming that men and women can be our best selves without divine aid, without grace, without faith. That being fully human is all there is; it is the highest level of existence.

How starkly this stands in contrast with humanity being created in the image of God—that men and women become our best selves in being doers of the Word, in conforming to God's will and God's likeness in Jesus Christ.

To express truly, with all our energy and soul, support for the rights of all human beings is a proper response to the eternal. But the tragedy of our witness is our effort to put human interpretations to all of life, rather than discovering God's meaning in our lives. This is why God sent Jesus.

Our destiny is not in our humanity alone but in recognizing that our essential humanity is our God-image. We are more than human; we are divine. Both our divinity and humanity depend upon our Creator-creature relationship. God is over us and for us!

Jesus the Christ came to be *with* us, and the Holy Spirit remains *in* us until Jesus Christ comes for us!

IMAGES IN LIFE

Recently an old friend of our family, Al, told me that I decorated her life. Flattering!

She said "decorate" in preference to the more familiar line, "You light up my life." It was her opinion that to say "light up" was to say the cliché or ordinary thing.

Immediately I began to examine her statement in the context of biblical proclamation, especially in connection with Jesus' words "You are the light of the world" (Matthew 5:14). From her comment, I gained the insight that a room flooded with light would indeed be barren without furnishing and decoration. So it follows that letting our light shine must be for the purpose of others seeing our good works, which decorate the world that our light illumines.

A POEM FOR AL

You may not be a mother
Who has carried proud and well
A tiny little baby
To make your body swell.

You may not be a woman
Who has nestled at her breast
A hungry, squalling infant
Who has kept you from your rest.

Yet still you are a mother
In, oh, so many ways!
For God gave you the precious gift
For which a mother prays:

The gift of fun and laughter
The gift of loving care
The gift of reaching children
That's really very rare.

Yes, God made you a mother
In the most important way—
The special kind of nurture
That you give every day.

So don't feel like a loser
And think you're really odd.
This day is yours to cherish:
You're a mother sent by God.

—VIVIENNE L. ANDERSON

IT'S ALL RELATIVE

The two very pleasant ladies next to me on the flight were chatting when the pilot changed gears on the DC 8, and one of the women commented, "It seems as if we just stopped. You can't even tell that we're moving!"

Of course, we were moving at twenty thousand feet up. Even if the turbines had failed, gravity would not have allowed us to be still! Thank God, the engines were rotating in apparent good form and the pre-landing systems were engaged. Nevertheless, anyone who has flown can identify with the sensation described by that lady. We did not seem to be moving because the gray sky outside our little window provided no relational object by which we could perceive movement.

So it is for many of life's experiences; there is no object of substantive relation by which we can predict or measure movement. We think nothing is going on and that we have nothing to shout about because we see life only against the dismal gray humdrum of our own isolated existence. However, those who are in a substantial relationship with Jesus Christ should never experience even the illusion of standing still. Rather we may have the assurance and awareness that we are continually moving toward the kingdom of righteousness.

JESUS LOVED HIM

Allan called to tell us that his son, Shane, had expired. Allan appeared careful to say "expired." Shane was only ten years old and had suffered greatly with leukemia for too long a period for his tender age. Although it was obvious that Shane's father was deeply hurt at the passing, there was also a tone of victory in his conversation. Both he and Shane's mother talked of the difficult aspects of their child's sickness, but they also talked of the strengths of that little man.

One night in particular came to Allan's mind. Shane undoubtedly had been in pain, but through it all had said, "Daddy, let's sing," and he raised the hymn "Jesus Loves Me." That response was in itself a gift to the family and a lesson to us all.

When I received the call from Allan that night with news of Shane's passing, I could not hold back the tears. Through them I meditated on Mark 15:34: "My God, my God, why have you forsaken me?" But I also remembered Shane's song, and I knew there was a reason why God had called him home: Jesus loved him.

NEVER THE SAME AGAIN

I guess it all began when I had a "near death" experience in August of 1981. I had had bypass surgery, which ended with complications. Three days following the ordeal I experienced the most excruciating pain, pain so extreme that I felt in it the tug of death.

My wife and my friend William were in the room. Both had prayed for me, and when I had struggled against the pain without result, I settled down to accept my unwelcome lot. Vivienne was rubbing my head gently, and in that assurance I faded into a state of oblivion.

The other side of existence was one of bliss and bathed in light. For me it was a time of ecstasy, the absence of pain, and complete satisfaction with my new environment. I had no desire to leave that pleasurable experience. Mine was a religious experience; Jesus was there. Then, amid the peace and beauty and satisfaction, the form of Jesus in a sort of miniature was lifted above my level and I sensed myself being returned to my former existence.

When I awoke, from there the journey to recovery was smooth sailing.

That day in 1981 was not the first time I had known pain of that intensity. Once was a result of a car accident, which I stoically bore; another was an attack of kidney stones which I felt I could not bear.

The only thought I had that second time was to be relieved of pain, no matter how; even death was not anathema. However, I was treated medicinally in a hospital emergency room and when I awoke the next morning I felt fine. It began to dawn on me that death is not an alternative to life; death is an alternative to pain.

With that new revelation, my experience in 1981 was different. This time, despite my excruciating pain, I had no longing for the release of death, for I knew ultimately the struggle is not to keep from dying; the struggle is to keep on living. In fact, with a new sense of hope, I was empowered to pray, "Lord, I don't believe you brought me this far to leave me." From that day, I've never been the same.

PAIN

A twinge here
An ache there
Darts within me uncontrolled.

My eyes glaze
Sudden haze
Hides the anguish of my soul.

My mouth speaks
Cheery cheeks
Greet the greeters unaware.

No one knows
Can suppose
Takes for granted all is well.

Oh, to see
Inner me
Struggling to be well again.

Unshed tears
Unsaid fears
Clamor for release within.

But who cares
Gladly shares
Feels what I feel, understands?

Goes the night
Comes the light
God is here; I'm not alone.

—VIVIENNE L. ANDERSON

ONLY A TOUCH

The television program *That's Incredible* presented a youngster who at one stage was, according to his physicians, within a centimeter of permanent paralysis because of a spinal injury. Spectacular medical care and the young man's own courage earned his story the accolade "incredible."

That story, however, involved another dimension which could easily have been lost. It was the simple witness of the youngster himself who, facing that monumental test, told the television audience that holding his mother's hand provided inexplicable support.

I have known such a touch. Devastated by the pain, trauma, and a measure of despair three days following open-heart surgery, I felt my wife place her hand on my forehead, an action that soothed and empowered my whole being. There was so much of her in that touch!

I am confident that touching by those who genuinely love emits a powerful energy. No wonder the woman with an issue of blood was healed only because she was able to touch Jesus the Christ (Matthew 9:21-22). Touched by pure love.

SEEING THINGS DIFFERENTLY

A friend and I were walking through the airport when I noticed a lady in a wheelchair moving rather smoothly along with no one manipulating the chair. The unusual freedom of motion was the result of the man walking with his lady, holding her hand, and as he briskly walked, so rolled the chair.

Pointing them out, I said to my friend, "Isn't that nice?" His response was, "That's a good way to do it."

How differently we had seen that action! He was being utilitarian, perceiving the efficiency of a technique; I was being relational, seeing love and care for a person who was differently abled. I saw in their countenance an unmeasured love, a creative love. It was obvious in the roll of the chair.

It made me realize how differently we each view the circumstances of our lives. Most of us tend to assess our experiences in utilitarian ways, considering only the practical movement from point A to point B. Thomas A. Dorsey has put it better in his lyrics, "Precious Lord, take my hand . . . Lead me on, let me stand."

SINGING IN THE DARK

For a long time I have heard the expression "whistling in the dark." The intention of the phrase is to depict a person's conscious effort to gird him or herself in the face of the shadowy unknown—or at least that person's attempt to impress the darkness (and whatever might be lurking in the shadows) with every appearance of contentment and confidence. In short, we whistle in the dark because we are afraid.

I've whistled in the dark, but even while I was doing it I was convinced that there was no protection in the whistling. The dark still seemed foreboding and ominous—well, not so much the darkness but the uncertainty of what was unseen in the darkness.

What we really seek to conjure in our whistling is an illusion of companionship—a sense that we are not alone. In our fear, we long for a dependable, unrelenting friendship that ensures confidence and faith. What peace we can have in knowing that, indeed, we can just "whistle" to summon our friend Jesus, who can usher us out of dark uncertainty and into "his marvelous light" (1 Peter 2:9). Then and only then will our fearful whistling break forth in joyous singing.

TURNING TO GOD

In my walk of life, there are always circles for talking theology, and often when that topic arises, naturally the dialogue revolves around what it means to be converted. We each can testify to the life-altering experiences that we have had with Christ, and usually none of us describes the process quite the same way.

That, of course, does not bother me, because I know the testimonies of three prominent apostles as they have been recorded in history. First, there was Paul (then Saul) on the Damascus Road, who saw the light from heaven, fell to the ground, and heard a voice saying to him, "Saul, Saul, why are you persecuting me?" (Acts 9:3-4). Then there was John Wesley and his momentous revelation at Alders Gate where, he wrote, "I felt my heart strangely warmed." And finally there was Richard Allen, whose eventful day he described in jubilation: "My dungeon shook, and my chains fell off"—a description reminiscent of the experience recorded in Acts 16:26.

However, there is another aspect of conversion that informs my personal experience and validates my sufficiency in the grace of my savior, Christ. Conversion is not a once and forever moment. It is more than turning *from* sin; it is turning *to* God, and the turning is the perpetual action of heart, mind, soul, and strength.

WATCH YOUR PACE

I was running late, but just in time.

I had awakened at 8:05 A.M., unnecessarily early for a 12:30 P.M. flight. I was sure I would have no problem snatching a few more winks and arising in sufficient time. I was wrong for taking that second nap, because I didn't wake up until 11:16. That gave me just one hour and fourteen minutes to bathe, pack, check out of my hotel, get to the airport, buy a ticket, and make it by train to that faraway gate at the huge Atlanta terminal. I did make the flight, by God's amazing grace! Yet, I also felt somewhat stressed in the effort.

I had fallen into the old pattern of rushing, knowing that I should not because of my heart condition. But old patterns are hard to break, whether internal or external. If we talk of physical or spiritual situations, it is important to set a pace for our life around the principles that have proven to be life sustaining. And what greater pace-setting principle could we have than that of following the Lord Jesus, who practiced waking up on time (Matthew 14:25; John 8:2).

WHEN THE ROOSTER CROWS

I was in Jerusalem on a peace pilgrimage with a delegation of church leaders. My body clock had not adjusted itself from St. Louis time (C.S.T.), and I had awakened between 4:00 and 4:30 A.M. In the stillness of the early morning, I heard the rooster crow twice.

My mind immediately flashed back to Jesus' words to Peter, his disciple, and I pensively anticipated a third crowing. It didn't come. Still, in my spirit I knew the rooster would crow again, and in every interval of the rooster's crowing, there would be another denial of Jesus. The good news is that, if we are faithful, Jesus never denies us (2 Timothy 2:12-13).

WHAT A BLESSING!

It was Christmas day. We had opened our gifts and everyone seemed pleased, but the highlight of the day was the sharing time during our family worship prepared by my wife, Vivienne, when each family member expressed what Christmas meant to him or her. The session was a moving time overall, stirred by the opening prayer done extemporaneously by Carlton, our third son. Randy, the oldest, was the reader, and the other boys, Jeffrey and Kenneth, the second and fourth sons, did instrumental selections with Vivienne as the piano accompanist. I was called on to give the closing prayer. Grandma Doris was the designated mistress of ceremonies and performed the charge capably.

But the real blessing and the greatest gift was the testimony shared by the boys. They seemed to be clear about the meaning of Christmas and how Christmas should impact their lives. It was a rewarding experience for us all and a visible sign that our whole family has not slackened in our trust of God and of his Christ. A shout had emerged among us. What a blessing!

PART III

of the role and
function of the CHURCH

I am having serious problems related to our efforts to stage an exciting event for the church. I am confident that modern media techniques should be utilized in the church's ministry, but what of self-serving motives? We would like to impact the nation with our church's story, but I am anxious that we avoid individual aggrandizement in pursuing our several social and political agendas. The church was never intended to be an exhibitionist institution, but a servant organism.

Jesus did not seek front stage, and when he was lifted up, it was on a cross. The church cannot lift itself by doing business as usual, nor should it flaunt itself merely for show. Our chief method in promoting the church as the body of Christ should be in obeying Jesus' words: "And I, if I am lifted up from the earth, will draw all peoples to myself" (John 12:32, NKJV).

THE AIM OF HIS SCOLDING

I was in a church setting where the preacher was deriding the congregation for being too quiet, hoping to rouse them to greater liveliness and vocal expression. Well, of course, liveliness in worship can be a plus, and one should allow the tempo in a service to fluctuate from high to low and vice versa. There are times when quietness just does not fit; then there are liturgical moments when loudness is obnoxious.

However, what really puzzled me about the preacher's scolding was the analogy he used. He suggested that if the congregation were in the ballpark, they would be spontaneously and loudly reacting to the proceedings. I find that concept curious, because I'm not sure the weight of that statement is honestly measured. For example, when we scold people for being quiet in church but loud in the ballpark, that rebuke is intended to evoke audible responses. We want to hear "amens" and "hallelujahs" and other expressions of praise. But that desire raises another question: Who is the object of that praise?

If the ballpark analogy is carried further, we must admit that there will be more than shouts of affirmation heard. Crowds in a ballpark also shout "boos" for bad management and errors in the field. The mood may also be characterized by "boo-hoos" when defeat is imminent for the eventual losers. Ballpark crowds are lively, but the noise is not always positive.

Should we really do church like we do baseball? Should our behavior in church really be compared to behavior at a sports event? I don't believe so. Praising God need not always be audible. It is neither person-pleasing nor crowd-pleasing, but God-pleasing.

THE ROUGH SIDE

Sunday morning the choir sang "We've been climbing the rough side of the mountain" as if bemoaning their plight, while stiffening their resolve to press on. And the thought occurred to me: If it were not for the rough side, we would never make it to the top. The smooth side is all but impossible to climb; there is no footing, nothing to which one can cling.

And, so it is in life's journey. Unless we encounter the rough and the jagged side of human existence and experience the hard and difficult places, there is no ledge upon which we can balance a sturdy and disciplined character.

If all we ever know is the smooth and easy side of life, we shall never build the muscles of the spirit nor possess the stamina of soul for the long and endless journey to eternity.

THE STRUT

In Baltimore, Maryland, the ushers in our denominational tradition, following the receiving of the offering, approach the front of the church in a style called "The Strut." It is a lively presentation of themselves as they proudly bring the gifts of the congregation to be consecrated. To watch them is a moment of inspiration. The pride, the precision, the passion engendered by their devotion to their task is infectious and admirable. Oh, yes! They strut to the rhythm and melody of sacred music!

Today I caught the spirit of those ushers as I trudged along on the treadmill doing my usual cardiac health exercise. My soul tuned in to the words and music of a familiar hymn, which put a new cadence in my step with every beat. My walk had been transformed from drudgery to joy, and I strutted, fully prepared to do the next mile and the next. When one enters the spaces of gladness with others, it opens the way to a closer walk with God.

THEOLOGY OR THEATRICS

Again the question of sincere worship was raised. Daisy, who is choir mistress in her local church, said, "I can't stand it when everything seems like a performance." The concern about faith versus feeling had come up twice before within a period of days, and the two pastors who discussed the matter with me cherish the emotional fervor of their personal ministry. They are both exciting and excited in worship, yet they see the flaw in present emotional styles that discourage diversity and choice.

I am indeed disturbed that there is too often too little substance in the current popular music called sacred. This is to say nothing of pulpit antics which are manipulative! I am convinced a shift has occurred from theology to theatrics.

There ought to be feeling in our religious expressions, but not if the result is merely a "feel good" religion. We have a tendency to choreograph theatrics rather than allowing a spontaneity that would have allowed more theological authenticity (1 Corinthians 14:12). It is difficult to be happy and excited all the time, and why should we pretend that we are? Isn't life both sunshine and rain? Theatrics try to shield us from reality, but the church should be a place where we can be real with each other and with God.

WHO WANTS TO BE ORDINARY?

I was with a group of church people who placed a great emphasis on being ordinary, and that bothered me. For some reason I did not want to believe that we in the body of Christ were intended to be ordinary. Ordinary is not a significant goal, and furthermore, being ordinary is somewhat relative. Who determines what is ordinary? And who settles for that when the extraordinary lies within the grasp of one's creative reflection and actions?

Ordinary is a psychological determination imposed on the mind by a culture of mediocrity, which is itself an external influence. To be ordinary is the way of least resistance. On the other hand, creativity comes from one's spirit and is marked by a restless yearning to be free. It is an intolerance for the status quo; it is resistance to doing business as usual. It is, in reality, a form of rebellion. Though reluctantly expressed in that manner, creativity is a compulsive response of the inner person.

Jesus Christ calls the church to creative and extraordinary tasks. To be creative takes courage and draws criticism; it is risky business. And, whatever else creativity is, it is undoubtedly the refusal to be ordinary.

REFLECTION

The older I grow
And the more I see
Of the struggle of souls
To the heights above,
The more this thought
Comes back to me—
That Jesus, the star,
Lights the path I trod
With love so limitless
Deep and broad
As he tenderly points
The way to God.

—VIVIENNE L. ANDERSON

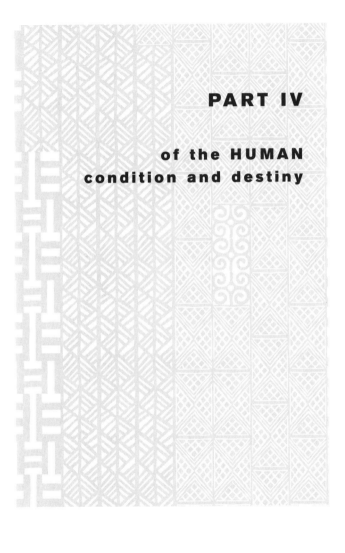

PART IV

of the HUMAN
condition and destiny

A CIRCLE OF LIGHT

Aboard TWA's Flight 228 from St. Louis to Dayton, I was reflecting on a rather troublesome situation when I engaged in conversation with my seatmate. He was troubled as well, about a relationship that was in jeopardy between two important partners who owned the company where he himself played a primary role.

He wanted so much to be the healer, if not the liaison in bringing about reconciliation. I shared with him a scenario that had recently emerged in my sphere of work, and he found my solution a helpful suggestion for his case.

While he was expressing elation for this new insight, I noticed in the sky outside my window a circle of light with the colors of the rainbow. This unusual phenomenon, one I had never seen before in my fifty years of flying, became for both of us a sign of hope. We had remembered the biblical story of the rainbow (see 2 Corinthians 5:18).

A REASON TO BE GLAD

The passengers for the flight to Philadelphia from Atlanta were all set to board at gate 33, Concourse C, when the agent announced, "We are having mechanical difficulty with the equipment. However, we have another craft ready, and you will be leaving from gate 26, Concourse B."

The passenger across from me exclaimed, "I'm glad I'm not going to Philadelphia!" A very innocent and harmless comment perhaps, but one which revealed the innate selfishness of humankind. We almost always think of self first. Had this man been truly altruistic, his first response to the announcement might have been, "I hope that the change will not cause anyone serious discomfort."

Aside from the fact that that passenger will probably not remember his callous comment, he will also not know how important going to Philadelphia was for those who so willingly made the adjustment that day. He had predetermined that the shift would be an inevitable burden, one he was glad to avoid, and he was uncaring of those affected by it.

In fact, many of those passengers traveling to Philadelphia were overwhelmingly grateful for the apparent inconvenience of having to trek all the way from gate C33 to B26; what one self-centered passenger viewed as a burden, they saw as an opportunity to reach their destination safely, with minimal delay. And they were thankful.

The reason we have for embarking on our ventures often makes the inconveniences along the way pale into nothingness, and our hurdles become inconsequential simply because they are milestones on the road to achieving what we desire.

A WIND MACHINE

Colleagues and friends often ask, "What's going on?"—meaning, "What's the scuttlebutt?"

Recently, when a friend related to me the news he had been hearing, I answered him by recalling a cartoon that highlighted the use of a wind machine. I suggested to my friend that much of what we hear depends on from whence the wind blows, and whether the source of that wind is an authentic natural phenomenon or merely a wind machine.

It may be difficult to determine the source or origin of all that we hear, but it is nevertheless a rather important perspective to gain. There are winds and windmills, wind machines and windbags. Who knows what is blowing in the wind? It is a waste of energy and much more a waste of emotional and spiritual resources to respond with seriousness to all the points of view that arise from pure speculation. After all, we are not to be "tossed to and fro and about by every wind of doctrine" (Ephesians 4:14). Instead, we are called to speak the truth in love, in order to "grow up in every way into him who is the head," our source, Jesus Christ (Ephesians 4:15-16).

AT THE JAZZ CONCERT

I was enjoying the music at a jazz concert with my lady, Vivienne, and perhaps for the first time, I really paid attention to the intricacies of this art form.

We had good reason to attend this event: our second son was not only one of the artists, but he was the promoter and producer of the show. Despite our subjective pride, the objective response of those attending proclaimed the performance of both vocalists and instrumentalists to be *par excellence*. As a jazz novice but a lover of good music, I rated that evening's entertainment as time well spent.

My great fascination was in observing how the musicians manipulated and integrated the tones into an orderly syncopation of melody and rhythm. They created sounds that spoke in an idiom relating to one's innermost feelings, and we in the audience were touched.

I saw in the work of those musicians a sign of God-likeness, for they were transforming form, beauty, and wholeness out of chaos. It brought to my mind a conversation with the deeply spiritual bard Howard Thurman, who talked about how one finds beauty by entering with rapture into those moments and places that have become sacred spaces for others.

My exhilaration at the end of the concert evoked in my spirit echoes of Psalm 150: "Let everything that has breath praise the LORD. Praise the LORD!" (NIV).

BEYOND GENETIC ENGINEERING

I am sure it is only a coincidence that my epiphany regarding the influence of genes occurred while on the Tuskegee campus, where the noted George Washington Carver's discoveries took wings!

I do not think my observation is in the realm of new discovery; I suppose geneticists could expound long and in-depth on what was for me an epiphany. It came on me with surprising impact and clarity. My sister Sharon, who looks like our mother, laughed and gestured in a manner reminiscent of the women in our family—so much so that in her laugh I heard Ruth and Faith, our mother and our aunt. Now what makes me certain that genes have an impact beyond physical manifestations is that Sharon's mannerisms and tones were not learned or copied from the older Anderson women; they had not lived long enough for her to know them.

There are, I believe, untraceable patterns ingrained in our humanity transferable only by an action of the Eternal.

BLESSINGS IN DISGUISE

The cover of the November 6, 1989 issue of *People* magazine featured what was referred to as a family photo of movie stars Burt Reynolds and Loni Anderson and their son. The magazine quoted Loni expressing their joy in the boy by saying, "Aren't we blessed?"

Reading those words, my mind raced back to a family who adopted a child nineteen years ago. They could not have articulated what the blessing really meant at the time of adoption; they felt only bliss. Now it is far more difficult to define the blessing. The nineteen-year-old is in prison, and pain and disappointment have crowded out the joy that filled them in the beginning. There is still a blessing in that relationship despite the bitterness, but it is not easily identifiable amid the clouds of despair.

Whatever the situation, we must hold to the testimony of James Russell Lowe: "Within the dim unknown standeth God within the shadows, keeping watch over his own."

DISCOMFORTING TRUTH

We all experience dark periods that we prefer to ignore. They are the days and weeks and months and even years when we really do not know what is going on in the lives of those we love. In our not knowing, we assume or take for granted that all we *hope* for is true. Or, we may think the worst and not wish to know the truth.

Then there are the situations when all of a sudden the light breaks through and pierces us with the discomforting truth. This truth can be shocking, like the naked eye is shocked when gazing into the sun. Then we learn that "Truth is sharper than a two-edged sword." It cuts, yes, it cuts, but—praise God—truth also sets us free.

DON'T GIVE UP

The only way to the parking lot behind the office complex was to drive through the alley. Under normal circumstances this was an easy maneuver, and the only possible glitch would be in not finding a parking space.

One morning I entered the alley and had reached an awkward position for turning around when I suddenly noticed a huge truck that from all appearances had blocked my pathway. In disgust, I thought ill of the inconsiderate driver and said of him, "How stupid!" I began to contemplate other options, but in the meantime, I was slowly moving toward my destination, only to discover that what had first appeared to be was not so. There was room enough for me to pass by because the driver had not been inconsiderate after all!

The position of the truck in the alley gave the illusion that it was useless for me to proceed, but the urging of my spirit signaled, "Don't lose heart." There are road blocks in life, and from a distance the way may look impossible or impassable, but we must not give up, for things are not always what they seem to be.

HOW MANY MILES?

Riding the exercise bike has become one of the routine activities of my existence. I began the program at the cardiac rehabilitation lab. Initially the process included a variety of prescribed aerobic exercises while being monitored for blood pressure and pulse by a competent medical staff. Having graduated from the program, I am now on my own, and I really miss the companionship of other patients and also the attention of the nurses. Their presence and conversation helped the time to pass more swiftly.

However, I have a friend who is also in the bike bit and who constantly asks me, "How many miles did you ride?" I was trained by the lab to observe time and reach a target rate for my heart, and so I had always ignored miles. Well, recently I decided to accommodate my friend's curiosity by keeping track of the mileage. In doing so, I am no longer a time watcher. The time goes faster and the miles become a goal to be attained. The lesson reminds me that life, too, is not so much about time. It is about the *quality* of life and of the goals we reach.

I DREAMED IN FRENCH

My French is really not so good, but following a trip to Haiti my subconscious images were reflective of my attempt to identify with the Haitian people. I had not realized that after more than thirty years I could make the language work for me as well as it did. Although I had a fair background in French in high school and college, I believe it was mainly my desire to identify with the Haitian people that gave me the recall I needed.

The people—so warm, gentle, and vulnerable—had shared a friendship that impressed me greatly. It was their patience which made it possible for me to sustain a limited intimacy that would otherwise have been unattainable. How magnanimous they were to me—never showing their pain or poverty. But, beneath the surface there is mystery.

That mystery invaded my sleeping hours when, hardly out of their presence, I dreamed in French.

VISIT TO HAITI, 1983

What do I see in Haiti?
I see the teeming populace
Of a raped and injured clime
Pushed and squashed into the mud and grime
Existing in the yesteryear.
I see the children, thin, resigned
Errant merchants on your heels
Insistent in their constant pleas
To buy their wares
No peanut-butter smiles I see
On babies dangling on the knee,
But haunting eyes and vacant stare
Wond'ring perhaps what brought them here
To this time, this place, this sphere.

What do I feel in Haiti?
I feel transported to another world
A world of captive, restive spirits
Enduring, biding, patiently waiting
Gentle, humble, proud, not hating
I feel incensed, repulsed, unworthy,
Angry, sad, defensive, guilty
Wishing yet with loving heart
As a mother feels her children's pain
To clasp them all in fond embrace
And make it better for each face
I feel a surging, joyous hope

That God is here, has not forsaken,
For whom he loves, he also chastens.

What do I hear in Haiti?
I hear the horns of automobiles
Racing against time on the narrow streets
I hear the donkey's mournful bray
Competing for life on the cruel highway.
I hear the deep unuttered cries
Of children groveling in the dust
With swollen bellies and innocent trust.
I hear the fruitless, pleading calls
Of those who desperately vend their crafts
Squeezed and crushed and knocked about
By countless crowds in the market stalls.
But I also hear the frogs, the birds,
Singing their thanks to a bountiful Lord.

What do I sense in Haiti?
I sense dismay, misunderstanding
Wond'ring how their miserable lot
Can be so different from the stranger near
With too many clothes and bodily pot.
Yet I sense no envy, no begrudging
Only a sigh, no blame, no judging
For deep in the wishes and unspoken hope
I sense they know their time will come

When God will say, "Enough's enough."
And grant them life, not tough, not rough
But freedom from th' oppressor's hand
For those who suffer in this land
I sense they know he loves, he cares
And hastens to answer all their prayers.

What do I say to Haiti?
I say to these my sisters, brothers
That I see, I feel, I hear, I sense
The wrenching pain of your longing souls
For in the falt'ring, labored step
The haunted, emaciated frame, a trap
For the birth and death of myriad dreams
That I, too, am you in various ways,
Trapped and beaten by impossible goals
I say your soul, too, is my soul,
Merged by One who made us all.
We march together, yet undaunted
Against dark powers of this earth.
Reach up, strive on, affirm your worth;
Hold out in faith until the dawn
For vic'try comes to all who pray
To claim God's promise—a better day.

—VIVIENNE L. ANDERSON

LOST IN VIVI'S WORLD

When I took seriously my wife's directive to find an item in her huge pocketbook, I realized that I had come face to face with an enormous task. I soon gave up on the search for the item she had requested, but in short measure Vivienne retrieved what I could not find. I began to think of her pocket book as a miniature "world" over which she has omniscience, and where I feel helpless and human. That experience was a reminder that even the little spaces can be awesome and overwhelming.

If we as humans can so easily falter in the small "worlds" around us, how can we not falter in our efforts to control God's world?

NEEDING ANOTHER

Vivienne's independence had greatly increased during my illness, which had lasted some fifteen months. She really pushed beyond her strength because she had discovered a major source of replenishing hope. She expanded the boundaries of her routine and took on responsibilities that normally would have fallen to me. And yet, upon my being discharged from the hospital, I found that she needed my help in a seemingly small and inconsequential way, because she had just had her nails sculptured.

When she had her nails sculptured, she needed *me* to do this, that, and the other. It is not always the big things that we do for one another that indicate our need for one another. Independence can never take the place of interdependence, for there must always be that modicum of the humane to connect us to one another's reality.

NOTHING ADDED

I am learning that talk has the tendency to kill sentimentality. If one tries to explain the inexplicable or to mitigate the mystery, then something is lost. At times, an internal thing makes the difference, not what we say. The sentimental is conveyed in some kind of unspoken language. Therefore it is the unspoken, the intrinsic, that seals its meaning.

We have often heard "the gift without the giver is bare." A gift given in sincerity cannot be measured in any form which places numerical value on it—not cost, nor weight, nor size. A gift given in love or appreciation can only be received in love or appreciation, no words added. The power is only in the giving and receiving. You can easily talk a good thing to death. What we mean is often far more than what we actually say.

ON BEING JUDGMENTAL

When Doris got no response from the lady to whom she had said good morning twice, the second time with great emphasis, Doris in disgust called the lady a fool. Having done that, she felt a sense of satisfaction. When Doris related the incident to us, it was Elsie, her sister, who observed that maybe the woman was deaf.

Now, whether the woman was deaf or not, that question put the matter in a far different context. It alerted us to our tendency of being judgmental and quick to criticize. We are not to judge others, lest we ourselves are judged (Matthew 7:1-2).

OUT OF THE MOUTHS OF BABES

When Vivienne audaciously engaged our grandchild Christian in what for him was a serious debate, "Granny" had met her match. For her, it was amusing to hear our four-year-old grandson argue his case, but for Christian himself there was nothing to joke about.

In the course of their conversation, Christian had used a word his Granny had trouble understanding. After she had failed to get it for at least the fourth time, Christian folded his little arms and said indignantly, "This is not working."

When Vivienne finally did figure out what he had been trying to pronounce, Christian's quick response was, "*Now* you're listening."

When children speak we must listen, for what they are saying may be more than what we are hearing. Hearing is critical, but listening is far more significant. For after all, it is "out of the mouths of babes..." (Psalm 8:2).

SACRIFICE OR SUBTLETY

"What is the real reason?" I was trying to fathom why my colleague, good friend, and roommate from college days would decide not to come visit for the Christmas holiday. He had said, "It's a matter of finance," but I wondered. It had been customary for our families to celebrate the holidays together at any price. Over the years, the depth of enjoyment we had shared always made it worthwhile. At any rate, we had always shared our resources, and it had never mattered whose wallet may have contributed more. It seemed to me that my friend had allowed a political disagreement between us to tarnish what we had always held as sacred—our friendship.

For me, Christmas is a time for celebrating the closeness of family and friends. I shuddered when a long-standing friendship appeared to be sacrificed at Christmas because of subtle professional differences. I trembled to feel that special relationship diminish. I would certainly have encouraged the coming of my friend and his family with the stroke of a pen, but my buddy refused, saying, "That would be charity." I think both of us knew such a demurral was a "cop out." That really bothered me. However, knowing that "all things work together for good" (Romans 8:28), I waited for "the good" to reveal itself. And for us both, "the good" eventually became clear!

SOUL IDENTITY

It does not matter that one's external identity is lost, whether by name change or cosmetic surgery or relocation or the sum of all possible outward alterations. There is a quality in life we interpret in our essence and in our deeds that cannot disguise who we are. What a person is inwardly cannot be erased by mere thought and cannot be buried by sheer will, for where a noble quality of inward life has ever found union between persons and where that quality persists, nothing is lost. The beauty in life never dies; the exterior form changes, but true beauty has neither color nor shape. It is as invisible as the soul. And because all else fades, only through the soul is there true identity.

SUPER SUNDAY

They call it Super Bowl Sunday, although I know that the Sabbath was never meant to be so called. And deep down, I wish they would not call it so. Nevertheless, I had to deal with reality: It was Super Bowl day and it was Sunday. For football enthusiasts, the occasion was a super event of super heroics.

That year was Super Bowl XVII, and John Riggins was the Washington Redskins' hero because of his tremendous rushing performance. Then, there was Fulton Walker, the Miami Dolphins' hero who provided thrills with his record-setting ninety-eight-yard run. Those two men, on opposing teams, after giving so much of themselves, were both winners, even though one was on the losing team. They had made it to the Super Bowl and they were stars, and so were their teammates.

There are no losers in life when we do our best. I have, therefore, rested my spirit on the belief that, when the Super Bowl makes that kind of point, then the day is about more than football. It is indeed a Super Sunday.

'TIS BETTER TO SEE

I had misplaced my eyeglasses, an occurrence which has recently become all too commonplace. So, once more I had the whole household engaged in a major search to find and to retrieve them.

My sons were still searching even as I located my glasses and restored them to their proper place on my nose. Then I overheard the dialogue between my sons in the next room as they showed benign concern.

"Did Dad find his glasses?"

"He must have found them; he's not down here looking anymore."

Well, they were right. I had stopped looking because, having found my glasses, I was now seeing. There is a great deal more virtue in seeing than in looking, and while there is a strong human tendency toward wanting to look better, our greater task is in seeing better.

WHAT WILL BE, WILL BE

I was in downtown Washington, D.C., with two friends at rush hour, and it was twenty-six minutes from my flight time. My driver friend assured me I would make it, but I did not see how that was possible. So, I silently resolved to take the next shuttle to New York.

As if to confirm this decision, my two friends soon made a prearranged stop at a shop where one of them leisurely sauntered in. Noticing the shop was a health food store, one of my frequent haunts, I followed, now completely convinced but resigned that I would miss the 5:00 flight. When our business was done, we were off again, arriving at the airport—to my surprise—with twelve minutes left before my scheduled flight to New York.

In times past, shaving my arrival time so close to the departure would have resulted in rapid heartbeats as I raced to catch the plane, but because I had accepted a reasonable alternative that another flight would be one hour later, I happily boarded the earlier plane.

God often works that way, I've found. When I accept that whatever God wills, will be, I am frequently surprised—happily so!—to find myself just where I had hoped and prayed to be.

YOU CAN'T FOOL ME

Uncle Arthur is a special kind of fellow. He is an uncomplicated, no-nonsense person who works extremely hard and is perennially dependable. Arthur never rushes, but always completes his task. His skills are those of an artisan, and he primarily works with his hands. It would appear that he never takes on more than he can handle, but he usually handles more than one job at a time. That way he's never bored, he says. He has learned the art of fixing the broken, while embracing the maxim "Variety is the spice of life."

Arthur's steady work ethic and calm spirit is accompanied by his wry sense of humor, which itself comes with a visage that adds to his comic demeanor. Arthur loves to chime in with one of his prosaic jokes, fully confident that everybody will chuckle with him. One of his lines often repeated is "You can't fool me. I'm too foolish!" Unmistakably there is nothing foolish about Arthur, unless we describe him as foolishly humble. He never claims to know more than he does, but he knows much more than one would think (1 Corinthians 3:18-19).

How blessed the world would be if more of us were like Uncle Arthur!

YOU CAN'T TELL BY LOOKING

Since those who might have observed from the inside of the building could only see and not hear the exchange of words, the impression could have been negative that day.

The gentleman with his wife in a wheelchair had asked me to assist in getting her into the car. Normally, I would have enjoyed being gallant, but this time I had to say, "I'm sorry." I was leaving the cardiac rehabilitation lab in the early days following open-heart surgery, and any lifting, especially in frigid weather, was a "no-no." Anyone who may have observed all of this from a vantage point within the building might well have wondered why an apparently healthy person like me had not aided the elderly couple.

I had become an object lesson to myself! You can't tell just by looking! My soul had a willingness to assist, but the flesh was weak.

PART V

of PRAYER and contemplation

A FAMILIAR PLACE

Recently I was in that big Atlanta airport again, but the place and my feelings about being there were different. The more I have experienced the sprawling facility, the easier it has been for me to handle. Of course, that's true of life as well; the familiar is far more comfortable than the strange. I've always known this, but it really came through on that particular day. I had boarded the train, ridden to Concourse A, ascended by escalator, and was a few yards from the gate when I realized what I had done. I had passed through all the obstacles, all the transitions inherent to flying out of a major airport, and I felt no anxiety, no consternation about whether I was making the right moves—I who in the past had always experienced such extreme levels of stress when traveling! I was now a part of that environment, at least sufficiently to feel at ease.

So it is as we travel life's journey. We are to seek and find the holy ground, the sacred and unknown territory, and make it a familiar place, a place where we feel a degree of comfort and peace. To know where you are makes a difference.

A PERSONAL PRAYER

Following my heart attack in November, 1980, I really agonized about what the future would hold for my health and what the implications might be for my ministry. In the hours, days, weeks, and even months after, I was still struggling to adjust. I had to take seriously the medical advice given to me, but I was also forced to find new ways to achieve goals.

Amid my anxiety to adapt, I sought the Lord in prayer, and the Holy Spirit led me to utter these words of release:

> Dear Lord, help me
> to persevere without stress
> To achieve without success
> To arrive without striving
> So that all that I do
> Brings glory to you.

It is that simple prayer which dominates my thinking, caresses my spirit, fortifies my soul, and orders my steps. I am forever reminded of my finiteness, and I desire that this prayer from my heart will quiet your heart.

ANSWERED PRAYER

Air travel appears to present my most opportune moments of reflective encounter. It was much the same on my flight that day in March 1998. As I sat in my seat awaiting takeoff, a passenger was brought on board on a gurney, with two medical aides who were constantly and vigilantly monitoring his condition with cardiogram and blood pressure instruments. Even as they secured their patient and equipment, in a rather abrupt turn of events the person appeared to reach a crisis point.

Having collapsed in an airport myself some fifteen years earlier, I was immediately attached to this anonymous fellow traveler. I knew he was extremely ill because the EKG indicated flattening lines, and I knew from experience what that meant. By now I had become emotionally but silently involved.

The medical team sprang into accelerated action, and a rather large needle injected some medication into the man's body. The patient's heart rhythm was almost immediately restored.

I was sitting near enough to note the low reading on the blood pressure apparatus (something like 97/51), however. My interest in the patient and the dedicated aides who tended to him had reached a deeply spiritual level, and I continued to intercede in prayer on their behalf.

It was one of the few times in my years as a preacher that I requested a particular sign from God. I sought confirmation that my prayer had reached its divine mark. So, in my heart I wished for the higher number on the blood pressure monitor to climb beyond 100. When after a short interval that number did increase, I knew my prayer was answered.

CEASING TO BE BUSY

We are constantly turning and stirring,
Convinced we can put things right.

Yet we have not satisfied the motion within,
And the cycle is repeated.

We are busy with busyness
And frantic with anxiousness.

If we could cease from unrelenting busyness,
Then our holidays
Would become holy days,
And our anxiety would be transformed into
    moments of rest.

For we shall not ultimately rest
Until from restlessness, we rest in God.

IN TUNE

There is a symphony inside of me
A drumming, strumming melody.
I hear it oft when I am still
When clamoring voices strive to kill
That surging, purging harmony.

Whene'er I stop so I can hear
The sweet bell tones so near and dear,
I sense the rhythm note by note
An inexplicable quote by quote
Of heaven's ringing, singing, tuneful band.

—VIVIENNE L. ANDERSON

COME HOME A CAPTAIN

The young woman ahead of me was boarding a flight from Columbus, Ohio, to St. Louis when her mother called for one last camera shot and then added, "Have a good trip and come home a captain!"

I could not help smiling to the mother. "That's a good thought," I said, a comment which opened a brief but powerful exchange between us. The daughter was a U.S. Marine who had come home for the funeral of her brother, who obviously had died a young man.

Before I could enter her grief, the mother continued, "Now she is leaving, my niece has died." My word of consolation was swift, but so was her turning away as she attempted to hide the pain reflected in her countenance.

I know nothing of that woman's religion, but her words to her daughter, "Come home a captain," had drawn me into an awesome insight. Despite her heartache, she still clung to a burst of optimism as she proudly informed me that her daughter had made the rank of lance corporal in just twenty-one days. Upon hearing that news, I understood the woman's profound optimism and I thought, "Why not 'come home a captain'?" That dear woman who wore no label announcing her religion, clearly exemplified an unrelenting faith. That day she was, for me, a captain of hope.

FEED YOUR SOUL, NOT YOUR FACE

I have noticed in trying to control my weight that the loss seems always to show in my face first. I wish it could be different. In wondering what I could eat to maximize facial stability, I remembered the phrase "feeding your face." I knew it was mainly a figure of speech, for feeding one's face may have little or no effect on the shape of the face—although excessive feeding of the face could change the shape of the entire body!

The truth is, however, that what we feed our face does very little for the center of the self—the soul. This takes a different kind of nourishment, which is spiritual. We may feed our face all we choose, but it will do little good for the self or the soul unless we feed also on the Bread of Life, who is Christ Jesus.

FROLICKING GRANDKIDS

During Christmas festivities three of our grandchildren were romping in the master bedroom with great vigor. The oldest, Natina, came running into the room declaring that Jordan, the youngest of the three, was chasing her. She called on the second oldest for help. In response, Carlton Jr. came hurrying to the rescue and wrestled number three down on the bed. Natina then indignantly ordered her accessory to get off the younger victim. Carlton Jr., the aggressor, objected, proclaiming, "I'm beating him up for *you*!" to which Natina retorted, "Well, be careful!"

Neither Natina nor Carlton Jr. had in mind hurting Jordan, because to them his well-being was important. After all, they loved him and were only playing! The older two were responding to the aggression of the youngest, but they were fully conscious of their parameters.

Perhaps we adults, in moving from virtual reality to reality, could learn from the children's attitude about caring for others. Even when it is necessary to scold, critique, or even more strongly discipline another person, love must be our primary motive.

The old adage says "You can catch more flies with honey than you can with vinegar." Of course, the more formal admonition is stated in Proverbs 15:1, "A soft answer turns away wrath, but a harsh word stirs up anger."

GRACIOUS

Clifton and I were traveling by automobile in Virginia from Roanoke to Norfolk, when all of sudden we heard a thud under the car. Immediately the motor went dead. As Cliff pulled to the side of the road, he was scratching his head and exclaiming over and over again, "Gracious!" He could not fathom this strange phenomenon that had impaired his brand new car.

Clifton is a very gentle, thoughtful, and serious person whose testimony is anchored in his own life to death to life experience. Some years ago, he had suffered a cardiac arrest and for an interval of thirty minutes, he had no heart beat. He had passed through that "valley of the shadow of death" graciously and had lived to savor the taste of goodness and mercy.

Thus, Cliff's *gracious* was more than an exclamation; it was a responsive testimony learned from a more serious time. So, naturally, in consternation in the midst of his present dilemma he was able to be calm and say "Gracious!"

HANDPRINTS ON LIFE

During my college days, now a half century ago, I was required to memorize Tennyson's "Psalm of Life." Recently I heard a story that brought those lyrics back to memory, particularly the lines "lives of great men all remind us, / we can make our lives sublime, / and departing leave behind us, / footprints on the sands of time." Now many consider the phrase "footprints on the sands of time" to be a curious metaphor since this imagery appears to connote temporality; footprints on sand are soon erased by wind and tide. Yet it seems to me that Tennyson was intuitively acknowledging both human mortality and immortality, in that we leave behind what we attempt to keep but keep what we are willing to give.

This insight took on new meaning when I heard about Eleanor, a schoolteacher who had gained a reputation by the quality of her students' penmanship. It was not what they wrote about her or even how creatively or eloquently they wrote in general, but that she had developed in them the ability to write always legibly. So, the word had gotten around that Mrs. Eleanor was a stickler for excellence in handwriting skill, and you could tell her students by the manner in which they wrote.

A man who had been under her tutelage was questioned about Mrs. Eleanor's reputation, and he reacted by asking for a pen and paper. After writing a sentence or two, he proudly asked, "Does it look like she might have taught me?" What a high compliment indeed!

Mrs. Eleanor taught her students to illuminate pages of their correspondence with a measure of proficiency and in so doing left behind handprints on the pages of life. How significant it would be if, like Madame Eleanor, we who are on this spiritual pilgrimage would leave handprints in life through the "students" (or what the church calls "disciples") whose learned qualities proclaim our own craft and commitment to the faith!

IT'S TIME

Never-ceasing Time
Has sped on
Its fleet feet
Covering the course of our days
In the places
Where we have shared as spiritual family.

But Time leaves its tracks
Deeply etched
In myriad ways
Marking forever
Our spirits—
Yours and ours together.

Time owes us nothing
Nor do we scold the years
For having left us
Just be glad
We've found each other.

—VIVIENNE L. ANDERSON

NO FAST WAY

Navigating the streets of Washington, D.C., can be awfully difficult almost any time of the day. As a comparatively new kid on the block, I continually searched for new routes from McLean, Virginia, where I lived, to the building where my office is located in the capital.

Like most drivers, I felt a sense of competence as I maneuvered the lanes with precision and appeared to be approaching my destination at a safe speed but with unusual facility. I was doing quite well during the morning traffic, feeling confident that I would be on time for my first appointment, when all of a sudden things got really hectic. Not only did the traffic flow slow to a snail's pace, but I had become sandwiched between a garbage truck and a fire engine, barely inching along.

Abruptly my drive to work had become more than just an arduous journey. Sitting between those two large vehicles took on profound meaning. These virtual mountains blocked both my forward progress and any thought of retreat or evasion.

But even as I pondered my predicament, there was an inward unrelenting of the spirit that quieted my anxiety, and I knew despite all obstructive circumstance that my mission would be accomplished. Indeed, I did reach my destination on time.

And so in life, when we seem to be on course and on schedule, the unforeseen rises up to meet us, and hinders our efforts to achieve worthy goals. Ecclesiastes 9:11 counsels us wisely, "The race is not to the swift." May we all find it helpful to pray, "Slow me down, Lord, and help me to make it to the Kingdom on time."

UNCONDITIONAL LOVE

When I question who I am and fret about who I'm not,
I listen quietly to you, Lord, speaking of
    unconditional love,
And I love who I am.

I love whom you made me to be,
What I am and what I'm not,
Because that's who I am and that's who I'm not.

Forgive me the sin of downgrading self:
Filled with your love sufficient
I will love without condition
All and everything you put in my life.

Teach me to pass on to others that love:
To love who they are and who they are not
For in your image you made us all
To love unconditionally and never not.

From the soul I shout unconditional love
To you, God, who made me and for all whom
    you have made
For the person I am and for the person I'm not
And for the soul I shall become.

UNEXPECTED DELIGHT

One of the great signs of love is in thoughtfulness expressed in deliberate care for the moment. My wife reads every label and studies every nutritional instruction to safeguard our health. She is absolutely incredible, both in her caring and in her culinary skills that are so creatively manifested.

When Vivienne recently presented me with a delicious, light and tasty delicacy for my evening dessert, it reminded me of a treat that she had often produced, but the texture was different. I believed it to be a new creation, so I called it "Vivi's Delight." But she said, "No, Clydie Reed gave me this recipe before we left Wichita." We had left Wichita more than twenty-three years ago, and Clydie had long since gone to be with God. But that moment of remembrance became a prayer of solidarity and thanksgiving for the life of Clydie.

How wonderful are the unexpected moments in which little things connect us to those who also care and who help define eternity!

WOODY'S ADVICE

My friend Woody, who had suffered a heart attack seventeen years before I had, called during my recovery to say, "Not to worry. You'll be all right." He went on to suggest that I rest every afternoon for an hour and a half, regardless of my agenda or the venue. It was his contention that nothing would happen in that interim that couldn't happen without me.

Although I have not fully complied with Woody's prescription, it was good and valued advice, and memory of it has altered my mental attitude. I have long since concluded that things will indeed go on without me and that what the medical community calls Type-A behavior does not guarantee success and achievement.

Thanks, Woody, old friend.

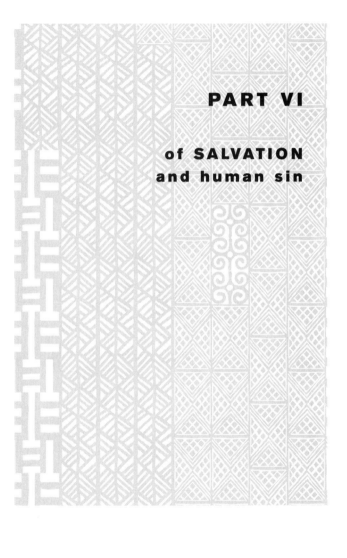

PART VI

of SALVATION
and human sin

A CROSS REMAINS THOUGH LOST

My briefcase was snatched from my possession in a crowded airport. That unpleasant experience created a strange emptiness in me—not because the contents of the case had enormous monetary value, but that it could happen as it did, and because that which was stolen had great significance to me and little at all to the culprit.

The briefcase's contents had included a cross that I had carried for nineteen years. Yet, although the cross is no longer in my keeping, its shape and image are so fixed in my mind that it will never really be lost. And because I cherish its symbolic meaning, which is the saving power of the cross, I trust that cross to affect the life of whatever person or persons may confront it.

There is transforming power in things when God has sanctified them. And so I hope that cross might invoke for those who touch it the words of the hymn writer Fanny Crosby: "Draw me nearer, nearer blessed Lord, to the cross where Thou hast died...!"

GRACE AT WORK

God initiates the covenant. God finds us; we do not find God. The human tendency is toward a God-complex—to act as judges in personal criticism of others. We see the splinter in another's eye while neglecting the broader issues of the community— and our culpability in those issues.

We seek individual salvation, believing our perceived righteousness sets us apart. We fail to acknowledge that grace can work even for the worst of us sinners. A personal claim of righteousness, while condemning others who may be in a different stream, is a kind of pride equally sinful as the shortcomings we perceive in others. God is the Emancipator, the Waymaker, the Way—and in Jesus Christ, God is the One who gives us all grace.

JIM AND I

I had been reflecting on the death of my good friend Jim, a bishop in another denomination, and on how enthusiastic he had been about the role he had played during the Quadrennial Conference of his church. Just two months after that chat, he was gone from our lives. It was so sudden, and he had been a comparatively young man, just in his mid-fifties. I, on the other hand, at about the same age, had been at the point of death with open-heart surgery but was spared to see a few more risings and settings of the sun. The contrast was a signal to me about the unpredictability of life and a reminder that I need not fret about my occasional aches and pains, no matter how serious they may be.

It is important for us to "press on toward the goal" (Philippians 3:14) in spite of what could go wrong. I have concluded, and know Jim would have agreed, that it is important to live life each day to the fullest, knowing the difference is made up not in what and who you are, but in whose you are and what you believe.

MALICE BEFORE THOUGHT

At a service stand one person said to the other, "The Jackson family is having a reunion. Aretha Franklin will be there and others."

The second person then responded dryly, "Whoopee! I hope we have to go to the penitentiary to visit all of them."

I do not know whether the person who made the retort was being flippant or whether this was anger, callousness, or disregard that was being manifested. But the comment hit me like a dart. Why? What had the Jacksons done to this person? I was sure there was no direct relationship. Is it that easy to hate?

NEXT TIME

Where will we be when we are in the same place? That sounds like an absurd question. I would have thought so until recently, but then I perceived the insight that we each must carefully ascertain whether we want to be where we are before we determine to stay there.

The basketball game had just ended, and the coach of the losing team was pleased that his team had made it to the tournament, but he noted that they had not capitalized on their breaks and had lost control at a crucial period in the game. Then came what sounded like a burst of optimism: "I hope to be in the same place next year at this time."

My immediate reaction was, "You can't mean that! If you are at the same place, you'll be a loser again!" What the coach meant, of course, was that next year he intended to make the tournament again. As believers, we need to be inwardly clear in our goal setting, because if we find ourselves in the same place in any striving, especially on our spiritual journey, it should be only by miscalculation. Rather than clinging to the loser's spot, we should realize we are here to struggle and to achieve, and perhaps next time to make it all the way.

THAT STILL, SMALL VOICE

That voice, deep within again,
Tells me all is not in vain,
Echoes from that depth unknown,
Measures all the deeds I've sown,
Finds me wanting, lacking still,
Trying hard to climb life's hill,
Cheers me on when I would fail,
Sets my course with ballast sail.
Oh, that always I could hear—
Heed that voice so soft and near!
Then I'd know the Master's will,
How he would my life fulfill.

—VIVIENNE L. ANDERSON

REAL BEAUTY IS INVISIBLE

I don't agree that "beauty is only skin deep." I think real beauty is far deeper than that—so deep as to be completely invisible.

Our survival does not depend on whether or not we are judged physically attractive. In fact, the least lovely parts of the human body are the "vital organs," the sight of which may cause the average person to cringe. Often, how one appears belies what one is, for our deceptions veil the reality and those lies are ugly even when our countenance is brilliant. It is the liar's charm which beguiles; true beauty does not betray.

True beauty is a quality intuited through vibrations originating in the soul. It is a virtue easily overlooked because it does not emanate from sensual perceptions. It defies sight, touch, taste, smell, and hearing to define its essence. Appearances are not reality. A thing cannot of itself be beautiful. Only a person can claim that soul-deep quality.

SENSING ARMAGEDDON

On listening to a TV account about a social issue decided by the courts and observing the extreme turnaround of moral positions, it suddenly dawned on me that our earthly sojourn has become more and more tenuous. To recognize the fact that one can hardly make moral decisions because of legal consequences is to sense Armageddon—not, of course, the literal version of a cataclysmic end of the world, but the slowly creeping, choking, painful grip of lifestyles so contrary to the biblical faith we have learned.

Armageddon is here! While not in all its fullness, it is still here. It is here in the manifestations of satanic human conduct, in our violation of the ecosystem, and in catastrophes that have resulted from human miscalculations and sinister motives.

The feeling of an impending end is often in our reflective consciousness, but for those who look forward "to the city that has foundations, whose architect and builder is God" (Hebrews 11:10), there is a better day a'coming!

SIMPLICITY

Does truth need to be embellished, or is it better served in simplicity? Does decoration give truth intellectual content or provide a value other than that which is emotional and cosmetic? How is truth improved? The dressed-up truth can be far more complicated to explain; the plain without the curves and bevels and inlays and moldings is much easier to comprehend.

And so I wonder: The masses of humanity are so uncomplicated. What is the intention of our Creator about that which is complex? Whose invention are words, the paint of our thoughts? Did God initiate them or are they fallen babble? Our theories and concepts can so readily confuse so many, and what we say is too often the opposite of our actions. I am resolved that the truth is best served by obedience to Scripture: "Be doers of the word, and not merely hearers who deceive themselves" (James 1:22).

SOMETHING MORE SUBSTANTIVE

I was making conversation with a little old man in a wheelchair who had been brought to the gate to catch a flight to Colorado and then was left alone to fend for himself. He said, "I need a skycap." And, of course, you hardly ever see a skycap near the gate. I offered to get an airline representative who could help him. However, the man insisted he wanted a skycap to help him do something in particular. I was using my imagination in an effort to determine his need when he took me up short by saying, "I want him to take me to the bar to get some drinks."

That man sorely disappointed me in wanting so desperately liquor to drink, and I immediately lost interest in giving him assistance. In fact, I began hoping that he could not find a skycap at all! But I also prayed for his deliverance from such bondage, wishing for him to find a substance more thirst-quenching and soul-satisfying, like Jesus Christ, our Living Water.

THE SELFLESS PARADIGM OF JESUS

The decisions we make ultimately become subjective responses. We choose to be on the side which is in our own interest. It is inevitably about my family, my community, my country, my church, etc. Self-centeredness is always the dominant determinant in human choices.

We have not yet matured to imitate the paradigm personified by our Lord Jesus, who in his commandment said, "No one has greater love than this, to lay down one's life for one's friends" (John 15:13). This model he ultimately carried to the cross.

When Jesus was tempted by the devil to jump from the pinnacle of the temple, Jesus said no. When the sons of Zebedee urged him to call down fire on Samaritan adversaries, Jesus said no. When Peter drew his sword in defense of Jesus in Gethsemane, Jesus said no. In every case Jesus said no to serving his own interests or to saving his own life. Instead, he chose to die that all humanity might be saved. The model for Christian decision making is Jesus, the Great Example.

PART VII

of social JUSTICE
and outreach

TWO SIDES TO VIOLENCE?

In the forefront of the apartheid debate was the issue of violence and nonviolence and the end thereof. But in any such debate, who determines from whence the violence comes? Is it the audible, visible actions of one who is in revolt? Or is the violence marked by a silent unseen cause to which the person is reacting? It is all too natural to pin the blame on the effect while overlooking the cause.

It is easy to see demonstrations and protests as forms of violence. On the other hand, for example, if one screams shrilly in an environment that is placid and contained, is not the noise magnified? Would not the effect of that outburst register as violence for those who had been enjoying the silence? Now, supposing the scream was the result of the irrational inflicting of pain by another whose action was silent and unnoticed. Perhaps the perpetrator had stabbed the victim with a sharp instrument and the victim screamed in the silence. Whose act was violent: the stabber or the screamer?

What I am suggesting is that the outward cry which has the appearance of violence could be a natural reaction to an insidious or unjust condition. The real source of violence is that which causes inward pain and diminishes personhood. Such violence wounds the human spirit; such violence affronts the heart of God.

CITIZENS OF THE UNIVERSE

There is a power which rises to put down all evil and bitterness and sin and hatred. It is that elusive passion and unity of the human spirit which is often displayed at the Olympic Games. Just when it appears that the wicked have taken control of the earth, a divine ecstasy bursts forth and rekindles the hope in our hearts. The tears, the pride, the patriotism, the camaraderie, the team spirit, the dreams fulfilled and unrealized—all of this was gathered up when the 1984 gold medalist Edwin Moses said, "I feel like a citizen of the universe right now." That is, indeed, who we are: citizens of God's universe.

DOES COLOR MATTER?

I couldn't help but speculate about the response of the couple who found a baby in their trash. Perhaps I shouldn't have done so, but I did. It was horrendous that such a deed had been done, and the couple both sensed it and said it. They felt so strongly about the incident that they attributed some good to be intended from the Eternal. A bad deed but a good omen for them—a baby at Christmas. They were committed to fight for custody of the child they had found. It was theirs with every breath it breathed.

So, was my speculation relevant or fair? Because what I wondered was, What if the baby had been of a different race or color?

HELPING OTHERS

Contrary to what some have asserted, affirmative action is not doing for others what they can do for themselves. It cannot be likened to a first-come, first-served situation. It is more like being at a table for a meal where most of the diners have a longer reach and are not strangers to the environment.

There is sufficient food for all, but the minority is disadvantaged by the slant of the table and a shorter reach. In that context all would be better served if a spirit of altruism was more comprehensive. This would cause the most advantaged to make greater provisions for the less advantaged. It is surely not about the lack of ability on the part of those with the shorter reach to eat or to appreciate the meal, or even a lack of willingness to stretch for the dish at the expense and inconvenience of the others at the table.

We must remember that the table itself has been slanted to the disadvantage of many persons by virtue of the circumstances. Those who occupy the seats of privilege must embrace the opportunity to level the table. Helping others is simply the human thing to do, following biblical advice that exhorts, "We who are strong ought to put up with the failings of the weak" (Romans 15:1).

HOLDING ON TO CHRISTMAS

We who truly catch the Christmas spirit try desperately to prevent the holiday from passing as just another day. There's such a build-up to that blessed celebration that even the commercials preceding the day remind us that something special is coming. And then, what? How I wish we could hang on to that Christmas feeling for 365 days—that is, the spirit, the exuberance, the hope, the sharing.

But, of course, Christmas creates some ambivalence, some paradoxes. It cannot do otherwise as long as the rich get richer and the poor get poorer. A while back I read a report that said money given to charity for the current year had far exceeded that given the previous year, and that was good to hear! For, "from whom much has been given, much will be required" (Luke 12:48). But, when philanthropy comes across as paternalism and personal satisfaction is perceived as its highest good, then charity becomes a negative force in our life and society. We ought not to give because it makes us feel good about ourselves. Whether we have little or much, we should give because there are needs greater than our own.

Since love is a higher principle, instead of placing so much emphasis on charity, we must be sure that our benevolence goes beyond handouts. We must be certain that our giving opens the way for those who are in need to find dignity in receiving, so that when they are given opportunities, they in turn will become agents of benevolence in someone else's life.

So, if we really want to hold on to the spirit of Christmas, then we must let love be the progenitor of benevolence, for love is "the more excellent way" (1 Corinthians 12:31).

JUSTICE, PLEASE

We were hurt and embarrassed when the car dealer called to say that we should return the automobile they had contracted to sell us, because their financial division had rejected our application.

Despite our impeccable credit record, we could not convince the dealership that the glitch was not ours and that the negative rating report was unfounded. The more we tried to clarify the matter, the more they treated us with contempt. Soon it became obvious that there were racial overtones interjected, and we were really incensed at this over-riding attack on us because of color. It did not matter that we had achieved significant standing in the larger community and held responsible positions; we were confronting blatant prejudice.

What choice was there but to stand our ground? For we were convinced that our struggle was for those who were less able to defend themselves against such bigotry.

We remembered the words, "If they do this when the wood is green, what will happen when it is dry?" (Luke 23:31). So we pressed our case and by the grace of God, achieved our goal, and gained a modicum of justice—profuse apologies and a major discount on our purchase. Nevertheless, the incident was a sobering reminder of the existence of systemic racism. Justice, please!

OPENING DOORS

Courtesy is commendable but not always practical. That thought emerged from a conversation about differently abled persons—commonly called disabled or handicapped. Someone commented about people who anxiously open doors for wheelchair citizens but who do not check to ensure whether the open door is kept sufficiently wide for the wheelchair to pass through.

That scenario illustrated for me a need for sensitivity to those who are different and their real needs, but it also highlights the problem of well-meaning individuals who point to opportunities for others without providing the assistance and impetus needed to help those others to achieve the goals envisioned. It is no good sharing news of a well-stocked lake if you have not provided accurate directions, offered needed transportation, provided essential equipment, and educated the hungry person on how to fish.

SHOESHINE WISDOM

Often, solutions to seemingly resolvable problems are found in places like the corner store, the local gas station, or in a recent instance, the shoeshine stand. It was the shoeshine man who predicted a decline of jealous husbands since the death sentence was now in effect.

I believe he meant to imply that a spouse would think twice about lashing out at his or her mate because the consequence of killing that spouse would be to suffer death at the hands of the state executioner.

While I rejoice at the prospect of fewer people being murdered in our society, somehow I am not persuaded that use of the death penalty as a deterrent is a truly Christian solution. Like the classic spit shine, the shoeshine man's prediction put the issue on display but quickly muddied it with a troubling solution.

We can easily become discouraged by such frustrated attempts to resolve this world's problems, but we may yet call upon the words of Paul who taught us, "Our competence is from God, who has made us competent ministers of a new covenant, not of letter but of spirit; for the letter kills, but the Spirit gives life" (2 Corinthians 3:5-6).

THE SAME OLD PROBLEMS

During the 2000 presidential election, Jackie was overwhelmed by the political fiasco and legal maneuvering around the vote count in Florida. She seemed to feel particularly incensed because it was happening in the state of her nativity and she would have preferred that the focus on her hometown of Tallahassee be for a far more positive reason. Nevertheless, she hailed the student protest as an appeal for justice and was prepared to stand with them.

Reflecting on her personal battles as a pioneer black student at Florida State University, Tallahassee, and remembering her father's legacy of involvement in the civil rights struggle, she recalled him saying, "Baby, I wish I could leave you a new set of problems." Noting her father's regrets, she bemoaned the reality of the situation thirty years later, exclaiming, "This is déjà vu! They're turning the clock back."

Sensing that systemic racism is still entrenched, she was hearing the haunting sound, "Don't rock the boat." But the deeper question, I believe, is about the moral fiber of our country and the ideals upon which it stands. To this I continue to ask, Will we recover from this political debacle and at what price?

WHO'S LAUGHING?

Is laughing a luxury? Can we really afford to be jovial? What do we really see to laugh at? Our world is so complex, and the responses to serious encounters are often inadequate or they are plainly ignored. Is there time to be anything but serious?

The facts that media news is seldom good, that the homeless and destitute continue to live on our neighborhood streets, and that charitable organizations persist in soliciting funds for needy causes are all evidence that something is desperately wrong. This overwhelming need of humankind describes our social condition and the hopelessness in our midst. Nothing's really funny about that! It's not a laughing matter. And yet, without a sense of humor we would go mad. Is there still a time to laugh?

I have the feeling that God is smiling at my consternation, even at this moment. And in my thinking that, I am laughing and thanking God for giving me something to laugh about.

EPILOGUE

from person to
spiritual person

I am a bishop in the church, but to me that is not prestige or power or honor; it is a privilege of service. My distinction is the same as that of every other Christian: first a person and then a servant of Christ. In the African Methodist Episcopal Church where I serve, we sometimes hear that "the power comes down," referring to the power of the bishops. However, power comes down not *from* the bishop, but *through* the bishop—down from on high from our Triune God, Creator, Redeemer, Sanctifier. What the bishop says, then, is not so much *ex cathedra* but *ex spiritus*, not authoritarian but incarnational, not directive but exemplary.

The term *episcopal honors*, which is often used in the A.M.E. tradition, inclines us to believe that such "honors" are a reward merited by service rendered rather than a wider opportunity for service to expand the faith and to teach the Word. The only honor a bishop should claim is the attempt to be faithful. Nothing else really matters, because no one relishes our apparent successes. They cannot, for it is a principle of our mortality to be selfish. It is in our redemption that we begin to see the good as part and parcel of the creation stream, and as the unique gift of each of us for the sake of all of us.

We can never be a whole unless all of us are a part—an inclusive identity, lost in a vast and comprehensive Oneness, a singleness implied in creation and redemption, in God, and in Christ. All of our words and deeds must flow into a unity, and by whatever means we struggle, we must find that common denominator to achieve it. Be it conflict or compassion, we must confront one another in honesty and integrity, with candor and with love—but face each other we must. Without that interfacing, whether in agreement or disagreement, whether in calmness or passion, no issues will come to the surface and no problems will be solved. It seems that no progress comes without toil and no accomplishments without struggle.

If the world is to be better, we will need to chart new courses, to ply new waters, to break new ground, to hold on to what's worthy, to be courageous enough to discard the obsolete and the fallacious.

We have done too many things our own way, believing them to be the only way, but all of us must learn the full meaning of Jesus' words, "I am the way, and the truth, and the life" (John 14:6).

In my personal pursuit of "the way" from person to spiritual person, I have clung to what I believe are two salient truths: First, that all humankind by nature has a bent toward sinning and that I am a sinner saved by grace; and second, that the change from person to spiritual person comes through faith in the birth, teachings, miracles, suffering, death, and resurrection of Jesus. Therefore, I am continually praying and trusting that I am on the way to perfection.